This book belongs to:

_____

To Charlotte and Clover, who have many happy
concerts ahead of them. With lots of love! ~ Beanz

For my mum, Gunnel, and for Gerda, Jack, Åse, Gerd
and Anne-Marie — women who made their own way in
the world, inspiring me to do the same ~ Jenny

First published in Great Britain in 2021 by Andersen Press Ltd.,
20 Vauxhall Bridge Road, London SW1V 2SA
Vijverlaan 48, 3062 HL Rotterdam, Nederland
Originally published in Australia in 2020
by Little Hare Books, an imprint of Hardie Grant Children's Publishing.
Published by arrangement with Rights People, London.
Text copyright © Davina Bell 2020
Illustrations copyright © Jenny Løvlie 2020
The rights of Davina Bell and Jenny Løvlie to be identified as author and
illustrator of this work have been asserted by them in accordance with the
Copyright, Designs and Patents Act, 1988.
Printed and bound in China.
10 9 8 7 6 5 4 3 2 1
British Library Cataloguing in Publication Data available.
ISBN 978 1 83913 212 4

HOW TO BE A REAL Ballerina

Davina Bell
Jenny Lovlie

Andersen Press

This is how you do ballet.

This is **not** how you do ballet.

Even if you think you're already pretty good,
you should probably go to a class.

Here is the
leotard.

It's like a swimsuit, but your mum will
not be pleased if you wear it in the pool.

Your hair has to be in a bun to do ballet.
This is quite hard if you have recently cut your own hair.

Bobby pins sound
friendly, but they
actually hurt *a lot*.

First position is not the first
position that you learn.
First you learn to be a
snowflake.

It's kind of boring if you are a serious dancer like me.
Just go with it for now. Same with the scarves.
You won't be stuck with them forever, I promise.

Step-hop!
Step-hop!

That's how I remember what skipping is.

When your teacher says
'straight legs',

that doesn't mean acting like a robot.
She will not find that funny.

My advice? Don't snip the ribbons off your ballet shoes and put them in your hair.

Here is second position.
Boring.

But here is third position.
This one makes you feel
like a dancer in a music box.

Pointing

doesn't mean sticking out your finger when you see something weird, like a seagull with one leg. It is scrunching your toes so they are long and elegant.

And the **barre** is not the same as monkey bars. If you make that mistake, you will spend some time in the Thinking Corner.

Sometimes the music comes out of a phone, but sometimes a real-life person will come and play the piano. She does not want to play a duet with you. (I already asked.)

First   Second

Isn't fourth position so pretty?

Third   Fourth

The best part is the concert.
It only happens once a year.

Before the concert, there will
be something called a rehearsal.
This is a practice where the teacher's
eyes pop out and her lips make a
sad rainbow. You might get to stay
late and go home when it's dark.

The bits on the
side of the stage
are called **wings.**
Pretending you have
wings is not allowed
in the concert.

But going on stage feels magic. Like fireworks.
Like Christmas-tree lights in your tummy.

And if you fall off the side, don't panic. People might actually like it. Maybe you could do this accidentally-on-purpose.

Maybe not.

When you can do fifth position, you will feel proud. You will forget how hard it was to stay still at the start. You will forget the time you had to spend in the Thinking Corner.

It might even make you
want to practise harder.

And if you are dancing
and your heart feels like
it's flying, you will
know for sure...

that you're a real ballerina.